INSIDE COLLEGE FOOTBALL™

FOOTBALL IN THE
PAC-10

ADAM B. HOFSTETTER

rosen publishing's
rosen central®

New York

For Mom

Published in 2008 by The Rosen Publishing Group, Inc.
29 East 21st Street, New York, NY 10010

First Edition

Library of Congress Cataloging-in-Publication Data

Hofstetter, Adam B.

Football in the Pac-10 / Adam B. Hofstetter. — 1st ed.

   p. cm. — (Inside college football)

Includes bibliographical references and index.

ISBN-13: 978-1-4042-1922-9 (hardcover)

ISBN-10: 1-4042-1922-6 (hardcover)

1. Pacific-10 Conference. 2. Football—West (U.S.) 3. College sports—West (U.S.)

I. Title. II. Title: Football in the Pacific-Ten.

GV958.5.P33H65 2008

796.332'630978—dc22

2007009612

Manufactured in the United States of America

On the cover: (*Top*) The Stanford Cardinal offense huddles up and calls a play to run against the archrival UCLA Bruins in October 2004. (*Bottom*) USC Trojan defensive end Lawrence Jackson (96) sacks Oregon Duck quarterback Brady Leaf (16) in a November 2006 game.

CONTENTS

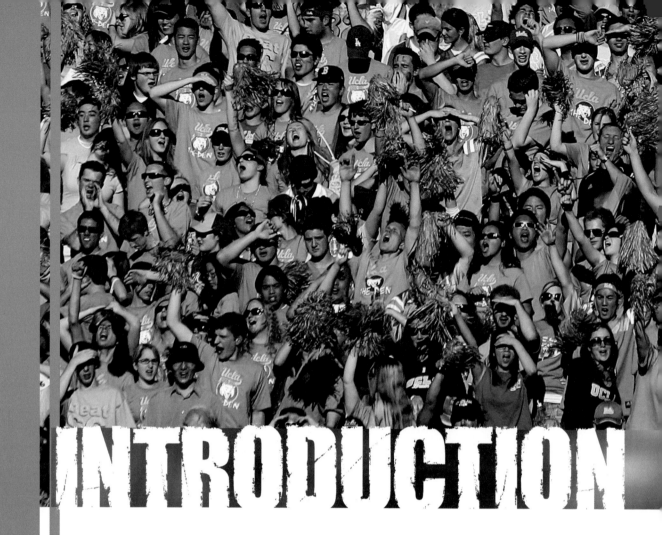

INTRODUCTION

Almost since the day it was formed, the Pacific-10 Conference has been known for great football and cherished traditions. Teams in the conference have been led by celebrated coaches, from old-school legends like Howard Jones, John McKay, Frank Kush, and Lynn "Pappy" Waldorf, to more recent field generals like Don James, Pete Carroll, and Mike Bellotti. Pac-10 teams also have been home to some of the game's most electrifying players, from Frank Gifford and O. J. Simpson to Troy Aikman and Reggie Bush.

But the one thing that really makes the conference stand out from all of the others is its rivalries. As a matter of fact, the Pac-10 is the only conference in all of college sports in which every team has a natural, in-state rival. There's UCLA and USC; Stanford and Cal; Arizona and Arizona State; Oregon and Oregon State; and

UCLA fans pack the stands of the Rose Bowl to cheer on the Bruins during a December 2006 game against archenemy USC.

Washington and Washington State. Those rivalries have led to some of the most exciting contests in college football history, including overtime nail-biters, big upsets, and some very unusual plays.

In this book, you'll read about some of the coaches, players, games, and even mascots that have made the Pac-10 what it is today—one of the nation's premier, elite college football conferences.

History of the PAC-10

The Pacific-10 Conference has been around only since 1978, but it has roots that reach back decades earlier. In fact, the Pac-10 considers the story of a previous conference called the Pacific Coast Conference to be part of its own history. But that claim is not entirely accurate.

The Pac-10's Predecessor

The Pacific Coast Conference was the very first organization for college sports on the West Coast. The PCC was founded on December 15, 1915, at a hotel in Portland, Oregon, by representatives from four schools. Those four original members of the PCC—the University of Oregon, Oregon State College, the University of Washington, and the University of California—established the conference to regulate athletic competition between the four schools. All four original

The presidents of the University of California, USC, Stanford, and Oregon meet on July 17, 1956, to discuss penalties to be assessed against Pacific Coast Conference schools whose football players received illegal payments from alumni and booster organizations.

members are now members of the Pac-10, but the PCC's charter was very different from the rules of the Pac-10, and a lot happened between the formations of the two conferences.

The PCC began play in 1916 and started to expand soon after that. A fifth school—Washington State College (now Washington State University)—joined the conference in 1917, and Stanford University became the sixth member a year later. By 1928, the PCC had grown to include Montana University, the University of Idaho, and the rivals University of Southern California (USC) and University of California, Los Angeles (UCLA). The conference consisted of those same ten teams until 1950, when Montana left to

Robert Sproul, president of the University of California, leads a 1957 meeting on PCC schools whose football players got illegal payments.

join the Mountain States Conference. The PCC might have continued ruling college sports on the West Coast to this day if it weren't for a 1956 recruiting scandal that involved several of the teams in the conference.

A Scandal and a Split

Throughout the 1950s, providing high school players with financial incentives to play for a particular school was a common and well-known practice. Although such actions are against the rules in college sports now, they were perfectly acceptable at the time. Fans who gave money to college sports programs were known as boosters, and those boosters often gave part-time jobs and even direct cash payments to student athletes.

However, some boosters got a bit carried away and started bidding on the services of the best young players. By the mid-1950s, several college athletes were being paid monthly allowances from the "slush funds" of boosters. Concern began to grow that wealthy boosters had too much power over the schools they were helping and that schools with less money were put at too great a disadvantage in attracting the top high school players.

In an attempt to keep the playing field level and maintain a fair amount of competitiveness among all the teams in the conference, the PCC made a new rule that no player could be paid more than $75 per month. However, the rule was not always obeyed. An investigation in 1956 found that dozens of players were being paid far more than the $75 limit. USC, UCLA, Cal, and Washington were all punished for violating the conference's rules.

What became known as the "Slush Fund Scandal" highlighted a growing rift

USC halfback Jon Arnett *(above right)* resisted the lure of professional money and kept playing for USC until graduation, putting his education first.

between the wealthier schools in the conference and the schools that had less money to spend on sports. With direct payments to players no longer an option, wealthier schools like UCLA and USC wanted to make the most of their financial advantage in other ways, such as offering full scholarships for student athletes, which was a relatively new idea at the time. Meanwhile, schools like Oregon and Idaho that were not as well-off wanted to institute conference rules that would minimize the financial imbalance among the schools.

With the teams' many differences in opinion highlighted by the Slush Fund Scandal, the PCC did not last much longer. The conference disbanded in 1959.

New Beginnings

The four California schools, along with the University of Washington, joined together in a new conference that they called the Athletic Association of Western Universities. Although the purpose of most athletic conferences is to organize competition among their member schools, the AAWU did not require its teams to play against each other. This unusual rule might have been a result of tensions left over from the breakup of the PCC.

Over the next several years, Washington State, Oregon, and Oregon State (by then known by its current name, Oregon State University) rejoined the group. In 1968, the awkward AAWU name

Success in Other Fields

Many of the USC's top players have gone on to play in the NFL, but the team's alumni have had success in other jobs as well, both in and out of football. Jeff Fischer and Jack Del Rio are not the only players who have coached NFL teams; Seattle Seahawks head coach Mike Holmgren was a quarterback for the Trojans, as was former New York Giants coach Jim Fassel.

Several other former players can now be found in the broadcast booth. Former quarterback Pat Haden does color commentary for some of NBC's college football broadcasts, while another former QB, Sean Salisbury, is an NFL analyst for ESPN. Running back Petros Papadakis, wide receiver John Jackson, and defensive back Jason Sehorn are all at Fox SportsNet. Former quarterback Paul McDonald covers USC games on the radio.

Lynn Swann tried to become the first prominent Trojan in politics but came up short in his 2006 campaign to become governor of Pennsylvania. However, one former Trojan was quite successful in making a name for himself outside of football. Before he ever appeared on the silver screen, the late actor John Wayne played outside line for USC.

One of the Pac-10's fiercest rivalries is that between UCLA and USC. Here UCLA's Adam Heater celebrates the Bruins' 2006 defeat of the USC Trojans at the Rose Bowl.

was replaced with a new name: the Pacific-8 Conference. Ten years later, two more schools—the University of Arizona and Arizona State University—joined the conference, and the name was changed to Pac-10 to reflect the new total of conference members.

Pacific-11?

In 1996, the membership of the conference almost grew again. When the Southwest Conference folded, the Pac-10 was interested in welcoming the University of Texas, a football powerhouse. Instead, Texas ended up forming the Big 12 Conference with three

CURRENT PAC-10 TEAMS AND THEIR ACCOMPLISHMENTS

SCHOOL	TEAM NAME	YEAR JOINED PAC-10	CONFERENCE CHAMPIONSHIPS	# OF BOWL APPEARANCES	BOWL W–L RECORD
University of Arizona	Wildcats	1978	1	13	5–7–1
Arizona State University	Sun Devils	1978	2	23	12–10–1
University of California, Berkeley	Golden Bears	1915/1959	13	17	8–8–1
University of California, Los Angeles	Bruins	1928/1959	17	27	13–13–1
University of Oregon	Ducks	1915/1964	7	20	7–13
Oregon State University	Beavers	1915/1964	5	10	6–4
University of Southern California	Trojans	1922/1959	36	45	29–16
Stanford University	Cardinal	1918/1959	12	20	9–10–1
University of Washington	Huskies	1915/1959	15	29	14–14–1
Washington State University	Cougars	1917/1962	4	10	6–4

other former Southwest teams and all eight teams from what had been known as the Big Eight Conference. With so much movement among the other Division I conferences around the country, the Pac-10 has held its current membership longer than every other conference but the Ivy League.

Looking Ahead

Today, the Pac-10 also is known for having some of the top college football programs in the country, as well as some of the most

MOST RECENT BOWL APPEARANCE	# OF PLAYERS TO WIN HEISMAN	1ST-ROUND NFL DRAFT PICKS	# OF PLAYERS IN NFL HALL OF FAME	# OF PLAYERS/ COACHES IN NCAA HALL OF FAME
1998 Holiday Bowl: Nebraska 23, Arizona 20	0	6	0	5
2006 Hawaii Bowl: Hawaii 41, Arizona State 24	0	12	3	1
2006 Holiday Bowl: Cal 45, Texas A&M 10	0	21	0	21
2005 Sun Bowl: Northwestern 50, UCLA 38	1	15	4	10
2006 Las Vegas Bowl: Brigham Young 38, Oregon 8	0	5	5	5
2006 Sun Bowl: Oregon State 39, Missouri 38	1	2	0	2
2007 Rose Bowl: USC 32, Michigan 18	7	30	11	36
2001 Seattle Bowl: Georgia Tech 24, Stanford 14	1	7	3	21
2002 Sun Bowl: Purdue 34, Washington 24	0	11	3	13
2004 Insight Bowl: Oregon State 38, Notre Dame 21	0	6	2	4

passionate rivalries. Those rivalries only will intensify now that, starting in 2006, Pac-10 schools will all play each other during the regular season. Nobody knows what else the future holds for the Pac-10, but if its past is any indication, then the conference will never lack for drama, excitement, or great football.

2 CHAPTER

Legendary Coaches

It's easy to focus on players when watching a football game, but the right play called at the right time can mean a world of difference in this game of inches. The Pac-10 has seen some of football's greatest coaches do everything from building upon already towering legacies to turning hopeless underdogs into mighty powerhouses.

The Golden (and Maroon) Age

In 1960, John McKay stepped onto the USC sidelines as head coach and ushered in a period of historic achievement that remains unmatched even today. Coach McKay led USC from 1960 through 1975. During this time, the Trojans won four national championships and fielded what many people consider the best college football team in history in 1972. It was after that magical 1972 season that McKay was named national coach of the year for the second time.

John McKay ended his time with USC as the winningest coach in history and was inducted into the College Football Hall of Fame in 1988.

In recent years, current coach Pete Carroll has carried the torch handed down from McKay. Since starting his career with the Trojans in 2001, Carroll has coached three Heisman Trophy winners (quarterbacks Matt Leinart and Carson Palmer and running back Reggie Bush) and has lost only one game by more than seven points. Carroll won the Home Depot Coach of the Year Award in 2003.

John McKay *(above left)* coached the USC Trojans for fifteen years. He went on to coach the NFL's Tampa Bay Buccaneers.

Turning Blue

The University of California, Los Angeles, first stepped onto the field as a member of the Pacific Coast Conference in 1929. Although the Bruins' coaches haven't had the same level of success as their rivals at USC, coach Henry "Red" Sanders did have a hand in how the team looks today.

When Sanders came to coach the Bruins in 1949, their uniforms looked a little different than they do now. At that time the team colors were gold and "true blue," or navy blue. Because Sanders

At UCLA, Henry "Red" Sanders coached the Bruins to three PCC titles, two Rose Bowls, and a national championship.

wanted colors that would look better on the field and in film, he decided to change all that. He began by adding the "UCLA Stripe" (a gold loop on the shoulders of the jerseys). He then changed the team's navy blue to a much lighter blue that he called "powder keg blue." Today, the Bruins owe their distinctively "explosive" colors to the keen eye of Red Sanders.

Wildcat Turnaround

The University of Arizona Wildcats have also had their share of disappointing seasons. During the 1990s, however, head coach Dick Tomey gave them a taste of what it means to be on top.

Tomey's Wildcats finished 1993 with their first-ever ten-win season. Anchored by their fearsome "Desert Swarm" defense, Arizona was set to face the University of Miami in the Fiesta Bowl. The Wildcats' defense had the game of a lifetime, shutting out the ordinarily explosive Miami offense for a 29–0 win and the first shutout in the twenty-three-year history of the Fiesta Bowl.

In 1998, Tomey led the team to a 12–1 season (a school record), going on to defeat the Nebraska Cornhuskers in the Holiday Bowl. When the game was finished, Arizona found itself ranked third in the nation.

Happy with Pappy

Lynn "Pappy" Waldorf took over a mediocre Cal program in 1947. However, Waldorf made sure that the University of California Golden Bears' lowly status didn't last long. From 1947 to 1950, the Cal teams known as "Pappy's Boys" won thirty-three consecutive regular season games. During that time they won three PCC championships

UCLA's "Pappy" Waldorf enjoyed three of each: undefeated seasons, PCC titles, and Rose Bowls. He also led Oklahoma A&M, Kansas State, and Northwestern.

and earned three trips to the Rose Bowl. Although the Golden Bears would end up losing all three Rose Bowl games, Waldorf would leave Cal with a 67–32–4 record and earn himself a spot in the College Football Hall of Fame.

Success in Oregon

The University of Oregon Ducks have had to fight to overcome their status as Pac-10 underdogs. Since Mike Bellotti took over as head coach in 1995, the Ducks have become a force in the Pac-10 and nationwide.

The Oregon State Beavers have seen a similar turnaround over the last several years. Between former coach Dennis Erickson and current coach Mike Riley, the Beavers have won four bowl games: the 2001 Fiesta Bowl, the 2003 Las Vegas Bowl, the 2004 Insight Bowl, and the 2006 Sun Bowl.

Washington's Winners

The University of Washington Huskies are another historical Pac-10 powerhouse. From 1907 to 1917 under coach Gil Dobie, the Huskies went unbeaten in sixty-three consecutive games and won thirty-nine straight games (the second-longest winning streak in NCAA Division I-A history). Dobie finished his career at Washington without losing a single game.

Don James took over as head coach in 1975 and led the team to two Rose Bowl victories in 1977 and 1982. In 1984, James's Huskies posted an 11–1 record, finishing the season by defeating Oklahoma in the Orange Bowl. But the best was yet to come. The 1991 Washington team was the best in school history and one of the best in all of college football history. James led the team to a perfect season, destroying opponents by an average score of 42–9. It was no surprise when the team won the national championship title. That year, Don James was voted Pac-10 Coach of the Year and won the prestigious Paul "Bear" Bryant Award (named for the legendary longtime coach of Alabama's Crimson Tide football team).

3 CHAPTER

Key Rivalries and Notable Games

The Pacific-10 Conference has been host to some of the most spectacular and infamous games in NCAA football. Its unique combination of in-state and regional rivalries, football powerhouses, and determined underdogs has produced years of memorable matchups.

Rivals and Roses

For more than seventy-five years, the University of California, Los Angeles, and the University of Southern California have shared college football's only rivalry between two teams from the same city. In fact, the two teams also shared the Los Angeles Memorial Coliseum as their home field until UCLA moved to the Rose Bowl in 1982.

As if that weren't enough, there's usually a lot on the line when these two teams meet: the Pac-10 Conference title, a spot in the Rose Bowl, and the chance to play for the national championship.

As a result, this matchup has become one of the fiercest of all football feuds.

The Game of the Century

The most famous of all UCLA–USC matchups took place in 1967, the same year as the first Super Bowl. The USC Trojans, ranked number one until suffering a huge upset by Oregon State, went into the game as the underdog to the top-ranked UCLA Bruins. To add to the excitement, the season's top two Heisman Trophy candidates, junior USC tailback O. J. Simpson and senior UCLA quarterback Gary Beban, would face off for the first time all year.

The Trojans controlled the first half of the game, charging into the locker room at halftime with a 14–7 lead. The Bruins were down, but not out. In the third quarter, Beban lobbed a fifty-three-yard pass to George Farmar in the end zone to tie the game at 14 going into the fourth quarter. Despite playing with injured ribs, Beban again found a receiver in the end zone, this time Dave Nuttall. The Bruins now had a six-point lead, expecting to make it seven with the extra point. The Trojans' defense stepped up to the line of scrimmage needing a big play. The ball was snapped, and Trojan Bill Hayhoe raced into the Bruin backfield and blocked the extra point.

The Trojans now had the ball with 10:38 left in the game. They soon found themselves at third down with eight yards to go at their own thirty-six-yard-line. If the offense was unable to gain the first down, they'd have to punt and hope their defense could stop UCLA quickly enough to allow the Trojan offense one more chance to score.

Anticipating a pass, the Bruin linebackers dropped back into coverage as quarterback Toby Page stepped up to the line. Page surveyed the defense, saw the hole left by the linebackers, and

USC's O. J. Simpson dashes through UCLA's defense in a 21–20 victory over the Bruins in 1967. Simpson would win the Heisman Trophy the following year.

quickly changed the play to a "23 blast." The center snapped the ball, and tailback O. J. Simpson took the handoff. Simpson veered left, and fullback Dan Scott made a key block. Simpson then cut back to the middle of the field, running sixty-four yards for a touchdown. The Trojans would nail the extra point and hold on to win the game 21–20.

Stanford and Cal

California's other big Pac-10 rivalry is between the Stanford University Cardinal and the University of California, Berkeley Golden

Bears. Nicknamed the "Big Game," this football tradition is more than 114 years old and remains the most highly anticipated and celebrated athletic event between the schools.

The Biggest Big Game

The Big Game has seen many dazzling finishes, but none have topped the spectacular game of November 20, 1982. It was the eighty-fifth annual Big Game, and Cal had home-field advantage at California Memorial Stadium. Although the Golden Bears were out of the running for

Stanford University fans hold the Stanford Axe, which is awarded to the winner of the annual Stanford-Cal game.

a bowl game, Stanford sat right on the cusp of a winning season and a bowl invitation. The Stanford team was led by star quarterback John Elway, who would go on to have a great NFL career with the Denver Broncos, earning two Super Bowl rings and places in both the College Football Hall of Fame and the Pro Football Hall of Fame.

Underdog Cal led Stanford 19–17 late in the fourth quarter. Stanford had the ball on their own 13, but it was fourth down with seventeen yards to go. With little time left and the game on the line, they had no choice but to go for it. Starting with a clutch twenty-nine-yard completion for a first down, Elway and his Stanford team marched downfield to get within field goal range for kicker Mark Harmon. With only eight seconds remaining on the clock, Elway called a timeout! If only he had waited four or five more seconds, Stanford's field goal attempt would have been the last play of the game. Instead, Harmon's kick sailed through the uprights with four seconds left on the clock. Cal would have one final chance to win the game, but their only hope was to run Stanford's kick down the length of the field for a touchdown.

Rabid Rivals

As long as there have been sports teams, there have been sports rivalries. When it comes to college football rivalries, the Pac-10 is the place to be. No conference has had so many for so long.

Although Arizona and Arizona State are the newest teams to join the Pac-10, their rivalry is one of the oldest in the conference. In fact, the NCAA has certified the Territorial Cup (which goes to the team that wins the yearly game between the two schools) as the oldest prize given for a rivalry game. The trophy was first awarded in 1899.

Oregon and Oregon State have no such trophy, but their rivalry is even older than the one in Arizona. The game between the two schools is known as the "Civil War" and was first played way back in 1894. Washington and Washington State also have been playing each other every year for more than a century. Since 1962, the winner of that game has taken home the Apple Cup, named after the fruit that the state is known for.

Perhaps the two biggest rivalries, however, can be found in California. Stanford and Cal call their annual game simply the "Big Game," and the winner goes home with the Stanford Axe. That trophy was originally a real axe but is now a plaque that lists the scores of past Big Games and is decorated with an axe-head. Then there's the legendary USC–UCLA game, which is so big that it doesn't even have a name. The winner gets the Victory Bell, an enormous old bell that was taken from the top of a locomotive in 1939.

Not wanting to give Cal the chance for a big return, Stanford special teams coach Fred von Appen called for a "squib" kick. (A squib is a short kick that usually goes to slow, bulky members of the opposing team who are not skilled at runbacks or ball handling.) Cal coach Joe Kapp, knowing that this was his team's last chance at victory, told his players to keep the ball in play by lateraling (passing it backward) if they were in danger of being tackled. What followed was so incredible that, decades later, it is still referred to simply as "The Play."

The Play

The whistle blew, and Harmon squibbed the kick. Cal's Kevin Moen grabbed the ball inside his own 45 and scrambled for open field. Finding none, he lateraled the ball to Richard Rodgers, who gained only a yard before he was swarmed by Stanford players. Rodgers then lateraled to Dwight Garner, who ran only five yards before he was swallowed up by Cardinal defenders. Before hitting the ground, Garner managed to throw the ball back to Rodgers, who then chucked the ball to Mariet Ford. Ford raced upfield to the Stanford 25 before he was caught by three Cardinal players. In a last-ditch effort, Ford threw the ball blindly over his right shoulder, hoping that a teammate—any teammate—would be there to grab it. Sure enough, the ball found Moen in the open.

Meanwhile, the Stanford band had seen the clock run out and walked onto the field at the Stanford end zone thinking the game was over. They were wrong. Moen rushed toward the goal line, dodging one Stanford player and outrunning another. Running right through the confused band, Moen crossed the goal line and famously leveled unsuspecting Stanford trombone player Gary Tyrell. Cal had done it! Despite the chaos, the play was ruled a

Kevin Moen of Cal celebrates in the end zone as the Stanford marching band scatters in confusion following the chaotic last-second finale of the 1982 Cal–Stanford football game.

touchdown and Cal won the game 25–20. Although the play inspired much controversy over the following weeks, the National College Athletic Association (NCAA) concluded that the ruling on the field was correct and Cal had indeed won the game. It is hailed as one of the most memorable moments in college football history.

4 CHAPTER

Star Players

The Pacific-10 Conference has produced some of the finest players in football. From quarterbacks to linebackers, the Pac-10 has seen history-making players come and go on both sides of the ball.

University of Southern California

When it comes to players, the University of Southern California is the single most successful program in the Pac-10. The USC Trojans have had more All-Americans, more NFL players, more Pro Bowlers, and more Hall of Famers than any other college team. Former USC players have played in all but two Super Bowls. One Trojan running back even is credited with speeding up the racial integration of football in the American South.

In 1970, many Southern football programs, like the University of Alabama, still barred African Americans from playing on their teams.

USC running back Reggie Bush poses next to his Heisman Trophy, awarded in 2005. In the spring of 2006 he was drafted in the first round by the New Orleans Saints.

When University of Alabama coach Paul "Bear" Bryant scheduled a game between his Red Elephants and the Trojans, he had no idea how African American running back Sam "Bam" Cunningham's performance would change things. Cunningham ran for five touchdowns, helping the Trojans dominate Alabama 42–21 and showing Bryant and other coaches what they were missing by recruiting only white players. Soon after this game, Alabama and many other schools integrated their football teams. In many cases, integration was due less to an idealistic commitment to civil rights and more to a desire to gain a competitive advantage.

USC has produced so many talented tailbacks over the years that it's earned the nickname "Tailback U." The name was first coined because Hall of Fame coach John McKay and his successor, John Robinson, produced top-rated tailbacks year after year from the 1960s through the 1980s. Leading the pack as the most famous tailbacks from this Trojan-dominated era are Heisman Trophy winners Mike Garrett, O. J. Simpson, Charles White, and Marcus Allen, all of whom would go on to successful NFL careers. Simpson and Allen, in fact, became two of the best running backs in NFL history

USC coach Pete Carroll congratulates running back Reggie Bush (#5) following a touchdown scoring drive against the Texas Longhorns during the 2006 BCS National Championship Rose Bowl Game.

and are enshrined in the Pro Football Hall of Fame. Current USC coach Pete Carroll has carried on the "Tailback U" tradition with 2005 Heisman Trophy winner Reggie Bush, who is now playing in the NFL.

USC tailbacks aren't the only Trojans winning Heismans, however. Since 2002, two Trojan quarterbacks have won the trophy: Carson Palmer in 2002, and Matt Leinart in 2004. Palmer was the first-ever USC quarterback to receive the Heisman, in a 2002 season in which he led his team to an 11–2 record and victory in the Orange Bowl. In 2003, Palmer was drafted by the Cincinnati Bengals, and sophomore Matt Leinart took over. With Leinart at the helm, USC went on to an

11–1 season and a Rose Bowl victory over the University of Michigan Wolverines. Leinart was drafted by the Arizona Cardinals after the 2005 season.

At wide receiver, USC's best known alumnus has to be Lynn Swann. Swann was known for his clutch performances, a reputation that he continued to burnish in the NFL. Swann won four Super Bowls as a member of the Pittsburgh Steelers in the 1970s and was elected to the Pro Football Hall of Fame. Today, he is known to a new generation of football fans as a sports commentator for ABC.

Offense may sell tickets, but most coaches will tell you that it's defense that wins football games. The Trojans' defense has had more than its share of Hall of Famers, including defensive backs Willie Wood and Ronnie Lott, cornerback Jeff Fisher (current head coach of the Tennessee Titans), and linebacker Jack Del Rio (current head coach of the Jacksonville Jaguars).

Although there haven't been any Trojan linebackers aside from Del Rio to make it to the Hall of Fame, USC has come up with its own way of rewarding them. The uniform number "55" has taken on special significance for Trojan linebackers, becoming a sign of defensive excellence. The Trojans' head coach assigns the number to the player he considers the anchor of the defense, which means that sometimes the number isn't assigned at all. Those who get to wear the number join the ranks of such greats as Junior Seau, Willie McGinest, Markus Steele, and Chris Claiborne.

One USC player who excelled on both sides of the ball was Frank Gifford. He was a star on both offense and defense for the Trojans and continued his success in the NFL. Gifford was elected to the NFL's Pro Bowl at three different positions: defensive back, offensive halfback, and flanker. He was named the league's MVP in 1956 and was elected to the Pro Football Hall of Fame in 1977. Even when his playing career was over, Gifford continued to make the folks at USC proud with his long, successful career as one of America's best known TV sports commentators.

UCLA

Among the most memorable Bruins players are Jackie Robinson, Bob Waterfield, and Troy Aikman. Although Jackie Robinson may be better known as Major League Baseball's first African American player, he was also the first Bruin to letter in four varsity sports. Robinson

UCLA quarterback Troy Aikman went on to be a star QB for the Dallas Cowboys, winning three Super Bowls and entering the NFL Hall of Fame.

excelled in baseball, basketball, and track for UCLA, and was named an All-American halfback for the football team.

As quarterback, Bob Waterfield led the Bruins to the Pacific Coast Conference Championship, went on to become the NFL's Most Valuable Player of 1945, and he was inducted into the Pro Football Hall of Fame in 1965.

Troy Aikman is probably the most famous of all UCLA players. Over his two seasons as starting quarterback, he led the Bruins to a 20–4 record and wins in both the 1987 Aloha Bowl and the 1988 Cotton Bowl. Aikman went on to play with the Dallas Cowboys, where he won two consecutive Super Bowls and set the team record for career passing yards. He was inducted into the Pro Football Hall of Fame in 2006.

Surprisingly, Aikman didn't win the Heisman Trophy. The only Bruin to win a Heisman Trophy is quarterback Gary Beban. Drafted

Pac-10 Award Winners

The following list highlights some of the Pac-10 players who have won national awards. While there are many honors awarded to college football players each year, the ones mentioned here are a few of the most prestigious. Many of these players have gone on to successful careers in professional football.

Heisman Trophy
(Nation's Best Player)

Year	Player	School
1962	Terry Baker	Oregon State
1965	Mike Garrett	USC
1967	Gary Beban	UCLA
1968	O. J. Simpson	USC
1970	Jim Plunkett	Stanford
1979	Charles White	USC
1981	Marcus Allen	USC
2002	Carson Palmer	USC
2004	Matt Leinart	USC
2005	Reggie Bush	USC

Butkus Award
(Nation's Best Linebacker)

Year	Player	School
1998	Chris Claiborne	USC

Bronko Nagurski Award
(Nation's Best Defensive Player)

Year	Player	School
2002	Terrell Suggs	Arizona State

Lombardi Trophy
(Nation's Best Lineman—Offensive or Defensive)

Year	Player	School
1979	Brad Budde	USC
1991	Steve Emtman	Washington
2002	Terrell Suggs	Arizona State

Paul "Bear" Bryant Award
(Nation's Coach of the Year)

Year	Player	School
1962	John McKay	USC
1972	John McKay	USC
1991	Don James	Washington
1994	Rich Brooks	Oregon
1996	Bruce Snyder	Arizona State

by the Washington Redskins, Beban was moved to wide receiver, and his NFL career lasted only two seasons. Despite his mediocre stint in the pros, Beban is enshrined in the College Football Hall of Fame.

University of Washington

Many of the University of Washington's most notable players come from the 1991 national championship team. The high-powered Huskies' offense was led by Rose Bowl co-MVP Mark Brunell and backup quarterback Billy Joe Hobert. In a record-setting regular season matchup with the University of Nebraska Cornhuskers, the Huskies' offense racked up a total of 618 yards, the most yardage a Nebraska defense had given up in thirty-five years.

Washington then rolled past the Kansas State Wildcats 56–3 in the Rose Bowl, holding Kansas to an unheard-of seventeen total yards of offense. Defensive tackle Steve Emtman shared MVP honors with Brunell, and he received both the Lombardi Award and the Outland Trophy, both of which are given to the year's best college lineman. Emtman later was named the Pac-10 Defensive Player of the Year and was the first player picked in the 1992 draft (a rare honor for a defensive lineman). Brunell also went on to the NFL, playing for the Green Bay Packers, the Jacksonville Jaguars, and the Washington Redskins.

The University of Washington also boasts quarterback Warren Moon as an alumnus. Moon currently holds the record for career passing yards for the Houston Oilers (now the Tennessee Titans), and the number "1" he wore has been retired by the Titans. Warren Moon was inducted into the Pro Football Hall of Fame in 2006.

A statue honors Pat Tillman, former star safety for Arizona State and the NFL's Arizona Cardinals. Tillman was killed by friendly fire in Afghanistan, where he was serving with the U.S. Army.

Arizona State University

Arizona State University had more players enter the NFL than any other school in the Pac-10, until USC surpassed them in 2005. Some of the most notable former Sun Devils include Jake Plummer, Todd Heap, Danny White, Terrell Suggs, David Fulcher, Darren Woodson, John Jefferson, and Pat Tillman.

Tillman went on to play with the Arizona Cardinals. He was remarkable not only for his talent and success on the field, but also for the bravery and patriotism that led him to cut his pro career short. Inspired by the terrorist attacks of September 11, 2001, Tillman left the NFL to join the U.S. Army. He and his brother, Kevin, trained to become Army Rangers and were both sent to the Middle East. Pat Tillman was serving in Afghanistan when he was killed by friendly fire on April 22, 2004.

Stanford University

Stanford has seen many of its Cardinal players go on to successful NFL careers. The most well known of these are quarterbacks Jim Plunkett and John Elway. Plunkett won the Heisman Trophy as a Cardinal in 1970 and was the NFL's Rookie of the Year in 1971. In 1981, he led the Oakland Raiders to victory in Super Bowl XV and was named Super Bowl MVP. Elway, like Plunkett, was the number-one overall draft pick when he entered the NFL. And, like Plunkett, he led his team to a Super Bowl victory and was named MVP of the game. In fact, Elway's Broncos won the championship two years in a row, ending a fantastic career that earned Elway a spot in the Hall of Fame.

Mascots

It sometimes seems like mascots are as essential to college sports as the teams themselves. That's no different in the Pac-10, where several famous mascots are an important part of their schools' athletic traditions.

The Disney Connection

One of the Pac-10's most recognizable mascots belongs to the University of Oregon. In the 1950s, athletic director Leo Harris made a deal with the Walt Disney Company to design a logo for the school's athletic teams. Disney did better than that: it agreed to let the Oregon Ducks use Donald Duck himself as their mascot. Oregon's version of Donald differs from the version seen in countless Disney movies and cartoons only in that he wears a green and yellow

Oregon shirt and hat instead of his usual blue ones.

Interestingly, Oregon is only one of three Pac-10 universities with a mascot designed by Disney artists. One of the others is Sparky the Sun Devil of Arizona State, who was created by Disney illustrator Bert Anthony. ASU did not always have Sparky in its corner, however. The team originally was given the unimaginative name the Normals before changing it first to the Owls and then to the Bulldogs. Finally, the students voted in 1946 to adopt the name Sun Devils, and that's how it has remained ever since.

Cardinal Red and a Giant Redwood

The Oregon Duck eggs on the home crowd during a 2004 game against visiting UCLA.

Certainly the silliest mascot in the conference belongs to Stanford. As if naming the team after a color wasn't unusual enough, the Stanford Cardinal chose a tree as their mascot. In 1930, the school's sports teams started calling themselves the Indians. The same Bert Anthony who created Sparky for ASU also designed Stanford's Indian.

That name lasted until 1972, when sensitivity to Native American students who were offended by the name led the school to rename its teams after the school color, cardinal red. The Stanford Cardinal (not "Cardinals") do not actually have a mascot, but the marching band's tree mascot has become associated with the school and appears at most Stanford sports events. The tree was inspired by the giant redwood tree pictured on the school's official seal. According to legend, it was chosen to poke fun at how seriously most other schools take their mascots.

Live Animals

One school that takes its mascot very seriously is the University of Southern California, though that has not always been the case. The school's first mascot was simply a stray dog that lived on campus. The dog was named George Tirebiter because of the way he liked to chase cars.

Since 1961, however, the mascot has been a pure white horse named Traveler. Whenever USC scores, Traveler gallops around the field, ridden by a USC alumnus dressed up as a Trojan warrior. The "warrior" who rides Traveler is often mistakenly called Tommy Trojan. That name actually belongs to a statue on the USC campus. Tommy Trojan is so beloved by USC students that, in the days leading up to the annual game between USC and UCLA, a group of them stand guard over the statue throughout the night to protect it from mischievous UCLA students.

Using a live horse as a mascot is one thing; using a live bear is quite another. When Cal's mascot made its first appearance, it was a live bear cub, a nod to the bear pictured on the state flag. After some trouble with the bear's behavior, the school decided that a student in a bear costume would be a much safer mascot, and in 1941, Oski the Bear made his debut. What's particularly unusual about Oski is that the bear's name comes from "Oski Wow-Wow," a popular, nonsensical cheer of that time that the students often yelled at games.

The Trojan warrior rides atop Traveler in the end zone of Los Angeles Memorial Coliseum following a USC touchdown against the visiting Washington State Cougars in 2005.

What's in a Name?

As uncommon as it is for a mascot to be named after a cheer, it's even more uncommon for a mascot to be named after a student. Washington State's mascot, Butch T. Cougar, gets his name from Herbert "Butch" Meeker, who played football for the school in the 1920s. Meeker was a talented local high school halfback but was smaller than most college players. When he didn't get any offers to play college ball, his high school coach started calling schools to recommend Butch. After first getting turned down by the University of Washington, Meeker found a taker in Washington State.

Butch T. Cougar, the Washington State mascot, was named after Herbert "Butch" Meeker, an overachieving Washington State star of the 1920s, who appears in the inset photo.

Butch Meeker soon proved all the doubters wrong by making All-American. He even got a chance to make Washington regret their decision when he scored a game-winning touchdown against them. That same year, the governor of Washington gave the school a live cougar cub as a gift. Because of Meeker's popularity, the cougar was named Butch. Eventually the school stopped using live cougars and now has a costumed mascot. One thing that hasn't changed, though, is the mascot's name.

Arizona's mascot, on the other hand, was named by a student from another school. In 1914, the Arizona football team traveled to Los Angeles for a game against Occidental College. An Occidental student working as a correspondent for the *Los Angeles Times* was covering the game and wrote that "the Arizona men showed the fight of wildcats." When the article made its way to Tuscon, the student body liked the description so much that they decided to use it as the team's nickname. The mascot that the newly named Wildcats chose was a live bobcat that they named Rufus. Nowadays, the school is represented by Wilbur, an anonymous person in a wildcat costume.

Mixed Breed

Although most colleges have stopped using live-animal mascots in favor of costumed characters, the University of Washington has both. A husky is a furry snow dog typically associated with places like the frigid regions of mountainous Washington, Alaska, and northern Canada. One such dog—a live Alaskan malamute named Spirit—leads the Huskies onto the field at football games. Since 1995, Spirit has been joined at UW games by a costumed character named Harry the Husky.

GLOSSARY

alumnus A graduate or former student of a school.

anonymous Of unknown name; someone whose name is withheld.

anticipate To look forward to; to expect.

booster Someone who supports a team or cause, especially by providing money.

chaos A state of utter confusion or disorder.

charter A document outlining the conditions under which a group is organized.

correspondent A person who contributes news reporting, profiles, analysis, opinion pieces, etc., to a newspaper or magazine.

cusp A point in time that marks the beginning of a change of conditions or circumstances.

dynasty In sports, a team that wins several championships within a short time period.

enshrine To place something within a shrine in order to memorialize a person, group, place, or event; star college football players are "enshrined" in the College Football Hall of Fame.

feud A bitter argument or longstanding rivalry.

Heisman Trophy An award given once every year to the best college football player in America.

helm The location or post of central control from which activities are directed.

homecoming An annual event held by a college or other school for visiting alumni.

incentive Some form of reward that inspires action or greater effort.

integration The bringing of people of different racial or ethnic groups together in equal participation, as on a team, in an organization or company, or in neighborhoods and schools; desegregation.

investigation Detailed or careful examination for the purpose of determining the facts of a particular situation.

lateral In football, a short pass thrown or tossed parallel to the line of scrimmage or slightly backward from the position of the passer.

mediocre Of ordinary quality; not superior; middling.

ploy An action meant to trick or frustrate an opponent to gain an advantage.

predecessor A person who held a particular position before the present position holder; someone who came before the present person.

prolific Producing something in large amounts and/or very often.

prototype The original or model on which some finished, refined product is based.

recruit To attract or enroll new members.

rift A difference of opinion or belief that causes a break in friendly relations.

slush fund A sum of money used for corrupt purposes, especially for the buying of influence.

successor A person who follows another in a particular position or office.

underdog A person or team that is expected to lose in a contest or competition.

upset To defeat an opponent who is considered better or stronger and is favored to win.

FOR MORE INFORMATION

College Football Hall of Fame
111 South St. Joseph Street
South Bend, IN 46601
(800) 440-FAME (3263)
(574) 235-9999
Web site: http://www.collegefootball.org

National Collegiate Athletic Association (NCAA)
700 W. Washington Street
P.O. Box 6222
Indianapolis, IN 46206-6222
(317) 917-6222
Web site: http://www.ncaa.org/wps/portal

Pacific-10 Conference
800 South Broadway, Suite 400
Walnut Creek, CA 94596
(925) 932-4411
Web site: http://www.pac-10.org

Web Sites

Due to the changing nature of Internet links, Rosen Publishing has developed an online list of Web sites related to the subject of this book. This site is updated regularly. Please use this link to access the list:

http://www.rosenlinks.com/icf/fb10

FOR FURTHER READING

Boyles, Bob, and Paul Guido. *Fifty Years of College Football*. Phoenix, AZ: Sideline Communications, 2005.

Bradley, Michael. *Big Games: College Football's Greatest Rivalries*. Dulles, VA: Potomac Books, 2006.

Braun, Eric. *Fight On!: The USC Trojans Story*. Mankato, MN: Creative Education, 1999.

Curtis, Brian. *Every Week a Season: A Journey Inside Big-Time College Football*. New York, NY: Ballantine Books, 2004.

DeCock, Luke. *Great Teams in College Football History*. Chicago, IL: Raintree, 2006.

Knapp, Ron. *Top 10 College Football Coaches*. Berkeley Heights, NJ: Enslow Publishers, 1999.

MacCambridge, Michael. *ESPN College Football Encyclopedia: The Complete History of the Game*. New York, NY: ESPN Books, 2005.

Ours, Robert M. *Bowl Games: College Football's Greatest Tradition*. Yardley, PA: Westholme Publishing, 2004.

Ours, Robert. *College Football Encyclopedia: The Authoritative Guide to 124 Years of College Football*. Rocklin, CA: Prima Publishing, 1994.

Pennington, Bill. *The Heisman: Great American Stories of the Men Who Won*. New York, NY: Regan Books, 2004.

Rockwell, Bart. *World's Strangest Football Stories*. Jefferson City, MO: Troll Communications, 2001.

BIBLIOGRAPHY

Cook, Beano. "Longstanding West Coast Rivalry." ESPNClassic.com. September 26, 2001. Retrieved December 8, 2006 (http://sports.espn.go.com/classic/s/beano_stanusc.html).

Farmer, Sam. *Bitter Roses: An Inside Look at the Washington Huskies' Turbulent Year*. Champaign, IL: Sagamore Publishing, 1993.

Fournier, Peter J. *The Handbook of Mascots & Nicknames: A Guide to the Nicknames of All Senior, Junior, and Community Colleges Throughout the United States and Canada*. 2nd edition. Leesburg, FL: Raja & Associates, 2004.

Layden, Tim. "Embarrassing Moments: College Football Risks Humiliation with Every Season." SportsIllustrated.com. August 2, 2006. Retrieved December 2006 (http://sportsillustrated.cnn.com/2006/writers/tim_layden/07/14/moments/index.html).

MacCambridge, Michael. *ESPN College Football Encyclopedia: The Complete History of the Game*. New York, NY: ESPN Books, 2005.

Mandell, Ted. *Heart Stoppers and Hail Marys: The Greatest College Football Finishes (since 1970)*. South Bend, IN: St. Augustine's Press, 2006.

Ours, Robert M. *Bowl Games: College Football's Greatest Tradition*. Yardley, PA: Westholme Publishing, 2004.

Quirk, James. *The Ultimate Guide to College Football: Rankings, Records, and Scores of the Major Teams and Conferences*. Champaign, IL: University of Illinois Press, 2004.

Wilner, Jon. "20 Years Later, 'The Play' a Tough Act to Forget." *San Jose Mercury News*, November 19, 2002.

Yarbrough, Roy E. *Mascots: The History of Senior College & University Mascots Nicknames*. 2nd edition. California, PA: Bluff University Communication, 2005.

INDEX

About the Author

Adam B. Hofstetter is a weekly columnist for SportsIllustrated.com. He has written several sports books for Rosen Publishing, including a book about the Big East Conference. When he's not attending various sports events, Hofstetter can be found in New York, where he lives with his wife and their two children.

Photo Credits

Cover (top and bottom), pp. 4–5, 11, 28, 29, 31, 34, 39 © Getty Images; pp. 1, 6, 14, 20, 27, 36 Shutterstock; pp. 5 (logo), 7, 8, 9, 26 © AP Images; pp. 10, 24 © www.istockphotos.com/Todd Bates; pp. 15, 16 College Football Hall of Fame; pp. 18, 23 University of California Athletics; p. 22 © Bettmann/Corbis; p. 37 © Icon SMI; p. 40 Washington State University Sports Information.

Designer: Tom Forget
Photo Researcher: Marty Levick